All our Hands are Stained
By Dwayne D. Willis, MA, MSW

To my Wife Nanette, my children Emily and Ian, and my grandson
Luke
From whom I draw my strength

FOREWORD

Ok, first question. What's up with the title of the book? Initially, I wanted to title this book, "Tales of the Syncopated Monkey." I'm sure you are curious as to why? Many years ago, long before I became "educated," as our society puts it, I worked in a Steel Mill, with a bunch of guys who were great. They smoked like freight trains, cussed like sailors, and were all certifiable. Most of them are now dead, mostly of cancer, but some had the luck to die from heart attacks or some other honorable deaths. One of them, named Pete, always would talk about that "syncopated monkey" headed for the front gate. We all remember playing with syncopated monkeys as kids. The monkeys we wound up and it just played the cymbals. Simple entertainment, of course, that was a simpler time.

Now we are adults, and our toys are a lot more expensive. But just like that monkey, we are constantly going through the motions looking for something to make us happy. We look for money, love, sex, power and other things for satisfaction.

I have been working on this book since 2012. But after watching my grandson picking strawberries one day with my parents he had gotten his hands stained by the berries, so I decided to change the title to its current title. I think it's more appropriate for all of us are responsible for our current state of affairs

My journey writing this book started 44 years ago when I started in the 1st grade. Until that time, I was the center on my universe. I was the only child until May of 1970 when my younger sister was born, (which I can refer to as the anti-Dwayne,) because even though she was brought up in the same household with the same loving working class parents she for some reason grew up to be a conservative Republican, and I through life circumstance, education and career choice, became very liberal. So I was a very happy child, until I entered the public school system. I was an overweight child as well as having problems seeing after an accident which burned my eyes (Quick actions by my father saved my sight.) I was also born with the grace of an elephant on roller skates. Within the first week of first grade I fell in a very large mud puddle and quickly became the source of teasing and ridicule of my peers. As I grew and matured became very articulate, but also was very lazy and easily distracted. I was AD/HD before it was a disease, LOL. But I use it to my advantage, I can multi-task like nobody's business, but like everyone else with AD/HD, I lose interest very quickly. Just don't throw nothing shiny in front of me.

Anyway, I digress. This book is MY opinions and my bitchings about a little bit of everything. Nothing is safe, so if you are easily offended, return this book to Kindle and ask for your money back. Foul language will be used. This is not for kids. This is not for stupid people, if you cannot think outside the box, turn off your Kindle and sent this back to the cloud. So if you're ready to think, let's get started.

Chapter I
WTF, MATE?

I had a mini-stroke in August 2011. After a CT scan and MRI, I was told that I had half a brain. What the fuck? I have two Masters Degrees! I am a retired psychotherapist! Anyway, this shit hit me like a ton of bricks. I cried for six weeks thinking each day was going to be my last. I have the brain of a person which had advance Alzheimer's. Finally I had to roll up my sleeves and quite whining and start copping my attitude of "FUCK IT!"

This capped a two year roller coaster ride which started on a nice August day at a residential treatment facility in southern Ohio between me, two colleagues of mine and an 11 year old kid. Now, a prone restraint, a ruptured lumbar disc and a crushed cervical disc for me was just the short end of the stick regarding my end of the deal. This was my two year experience involving Worker's Compensation. Now for you folks who do not understand anything about Worker's Comp, let me take a moment to give you a crash course in it. As a worker (any worker,) you are supposed to be protected when you are injured or worse killed on the job. WRONG. The minute you file your claim, they start finding ways to deny the claim. Mine was an injury which occurred while assisting in a restraint of an 11 year old boy who was going to injure two of my co-workers by kicking them in the head. When I attempted to get his legs under control, I came away with a ruptured disc in my lower back and in my neck. Saved two, sacrificed one, pretty good deal if you asked me.

After countless MRIs, CT scans, physical exams, doctor visits, and hearings before administrative law judges, I had to get surgery done on my back with my commercial insurance.

Hmmmmm. Who got screwed? And then I applied for Social Security Disability, which is an entirely different level battle. Now, as a social worker, if I had said I had a chronic mental illness, such as Bi-polar disorder, Schizophrenia, or some of the nasty mental illnesses described in the DSM-IV TR, I would have went to the head of the class, and received my "crazy check." Oh, did I mention that if you are offended by anything in the book, close it, delete it, and get it when you grow up. This book is for grown-ups. I cuss. I get pissed off. I have strong opinions and am not afraid to speak my mind.

About 15 years ago, state legislatures "reformed" worker's compensations to make it more "business friendly." Hint: "Business Friendly" is a code word for screwing the worker. I got screwed, but in the end, after the only people who believing me was my two children and my parents, I finally won my battle. Worker's Comp and Social Security settled with me. I had my surgery, I quit falling uncontrollably and regained control of my bodily functions. As of the writing of this book, I suffered nerve damage which requires an additional surgery to install a spinal cord stimulator to stop the pain I still suffer. So now I have returned to work and am pretty happy. But, I am still concerned regarding the power in which business now has over the working man. Years ago, there was an unwritten social contract between those in management and those who actually "made" stuff. You worked for thirty years at a job and in the end of that time, you got a nice pension and a gold watch for your dedicated service. Sometime in the 1970's or early 1980's, someone decided that it would be just a wonderful idea that America wasn't such a good place to make stuff anymore. American workers were too well paid and enjoyed too many benefits. Worker's Comp being one of them.

People think that workers set out to get intentionally hurt, so they can live receiving cash and medical care for free for the rest of their lives, right? WRONG! When you are hurt, can't work and are in pain, you want nothing more than to have your old life back. When you could do things, play with your grandkids, do little odd jobs around the house or even mow your own grass. Trust me, Doctor Visits and surgery consults are not my interpretation of "living off the dole."

Chapter II

OF ALL THE THINGS I'VE LOST I MISS MY YOUTH
THE MOST

Let's face it, not matter how hard we try to avoid it, we all get old. Our grandparents and great-grandparents aged with the grace and dignity that I still remember to this day. But we baby boomers, FUCK NO! From Viagra to boob jobs to face lifts to Botox. We baby boomers fight aging like a fucking prize fighter. We have now Seniors still behaving much like they did when they were in their twenties back in the 1960s. Guess what kids? You are they exact people are now responsible for fucking up the environment and economy as well as a whole lot of shit that now your children and grandchildren are going to have to deal with. And guess what? No matter how hard you attempt to fight the hands of time, you are going to lose. In other words, YOU ARE GOING TO DIE!!! So deal with it!

Remember, it was you all who thought it was such a wonderful brilliant idea to put Ronald Reagan in the White House, setting up the systematic dismantling of the middle class over the past 30 plus years. The wages over the top wealthiest 1% of Americans has steadily increased while the wages of the bottom 99% have remained stagnant or declined, depending upon the level of your income. What really pisses me off about my generation (yes, regrettably I came in on the tail end of the baby boomers, being born in 1964,) is the fact that we are the most selfish, most materialistic, most over protective of your kids of any generation in the history of the United States. It was your generation who created junk bonds, leveraged buyouts, the "mommy track, and a whole host of philosophies which took America from the King of the Hill to no more than a service oriented bottom feeder. And your reward for your scorched earth business acumen? A 401K worth half its value, your kids living in your basement after graduating college working at McDonald's with a giant Student loan payment hanging over their heads! Congratulations, you've achieved the American Capitalist dream of fucking everyone to make a profit but in process wound up screwing yourself!

Do I seem angry and vindictive about my generation? Indeed I do. During the 1960's, they took John F. Kennedy's line of "Ask not what you can do for your country?" and perverted it to, "What's in it for me?" They took our society and started glorified youth, beauty, and sex. It is an established fact, that since the advent of the birth control pill and then Roe V. Wade in 1973, the rate of teen pregnancy has risen during the 1970's, and 1980's. So much for the neo-con argument that access to abortion impacts teen pregnancy. Bullshit. But that is an argument for another chapter in this book.

As I said previously, the baby boomers were the first generation to glorify youth, beauty, sexuality, as well as the anti-hero. They introduced us to Cool Hand Luke, Dog Day Afternoon, Billy Jack, and a whole host of folks who lived just on the fringes of society. Of course, they also brought us Charlie Manson, Jim Jones and a whole host of other evil characters. They told us never to trust anyone over 30, but what happened when they turned 40? I remember reading in Time and Newsweek that Baby Boomer would be a force to be reckoned with. With their MBA's and business savvy, they would turn America upside down. And boy, were they ever correct. In just a few short years, we from a country that made things to a country that pushed paper, by that I mean stocks and bonds. But I digress.

By youth and beauty worship, today in the 21th century, look around. Look at MTV and VH1, which back in the day (my day,) they actually played music, Now I don't know what the hell they exist for except to show how stupid today's teenagers and twenty-somethings are. But so as you sow as you shall you reap. Now a couple of the young people in Buckwild are in jail awaiting trial on drug charges. Nothing like good old perpetuation of a stereotype. Of course, this brings me back to my original point of how the baby boomers destroyed the economy for future generations. American used to make things, my grandfather was a good old school Union steelworker, and my father was a Union Railroad engineer. Both of them did not want their children to grow up working in hot dirty dangerous environments that they had to work in, they wanted the better life for their kids, they wanted their kids to grow up and go to college. I went to college before dropping out (or being kicked out) and going to work for the same steel mill my grandfather my grandfather worked in for 30 years. It was the best 5 years of employment I had before I became a social worker. Yes, it was hot, dirty and dangerous, but I loved it. And I decided that it was worthy of work for the rest of my natural life. But it was not to be. Somewhere, someone who did not know me decided that my work place was old, outdated and destined for downsizing. So in 1992, I and 1500 of my union brothers and sisters were shown the door. With a wife, a mortgage, a daughter and a son on the way, I did what any normal person would do, I went to college. Actually, I show the handwriting on the wall about a year before and started college studies then. I took classes like a man possessed, taking and finishing classes a record time.

So did my efforts pay off with my freshly minted BBA? Hell, no! I had to endure two years' worth of unemployment before accepting a position as a controller at a construction company 45 minutes from home. It was a good job under a man who was a self-made millionaire. For the two years I worked for him and his family, I became very close to his family (and while I worked through my first graduate degree,) and established on thing that was more precious than either the pay or experience I received during that time. And that was trust. The man trusted me to handle literally hundreds of thousands of dollars both coming in and out of his operation. That honor was more precious to me than gold. The owner of that company past away in January, 2011 of a Massive heart attack while on vacation in Florida with his wife of 56 years. He earned the vacation. And he was an honorable man. He supported me while I was trying to reinvent myself and better myself with my education.

My major gripe with today's economy is the fact that those who sit in cushy office have the attitude believe that if only a person is motivated and driven, they will be a success. But there is a lot more to it that figures into the equation. People get sick, their children get sick, cars break down, and a whole host of other obstacles crop up. Employers nowadays have very strict policies concerning attendance, and if you violate attendance policies, you are gone. Do not pass go, do not collect $200. Of course they mark it up to a lack of work ethic and wanting something and not willing to work for it. This is a horrid and callous way to look at our future. But these are the children and grandchildren of the Baby Boomer generation. They were spoiled, their parents were too focused on their careers to give them love, attention and direction they needed in which they need to develop a proper work ethic. They left that to teachers, ministers, and other surrogate parents who operated *in loco partenis.*

Of course, I do not blame the Baby Boomers for being a bunch of mindless selfish bastards. Wait a minute, strike that. I DO! No one generation has done more to literally fuck up, trash, destroy, decimate and otherwise screw up not only our economy, but our environment and pretty much everything else they've touched all in the name of pure greed. They lived up the character Gordon Gecko in the movie, *Wall Street*, when he said, "Greed, for lack of a better word, is good." Trust me, when I was a business student at the University of Kentucky in the mid-1980s, I saw first-hand what was being produced. A bunch of consumers. Indeed. Nothing more than a bunch of mindless drones who were being taught first how to screw everyone to make a profit (or sell,) and second to take their gains and spend it on nice cars and houses, to get their version of the American Dream. I seriously wonder if those kids of long ago ever grew a conscience. Anyway, enough of this bullshit. Time for me to go Academic. Yes, not only am I pissed off at American and the way our elected leaders have decided to crap on its citizens. I'm even madder at its citizens for being gullible enough to allow it to happen to them. So in the next few chapters I am going to show you how corporate downsizing became a matter of public policy. Hopefully this will get someone mad enough to do something instead of just sitting idly by and letting the train run over you.

CHAPTER III

HERE'S HOW THE MONKEY (AND THE REST OF US)
GOT THE SCREW.

Once upon a time, not too long ago, but so far ago that no one under the age of 25 can remember it, that a young person in this country could graduate from high school (or college, if one was so inclined) and almost immediately go to work for an employer with the understanding that after 30 or 40 years of faithful service to the company, he would receive a gold watch, a retirement party, and a nice pension in which he and his spouse could live comfortably in their "golden years." This was given in exchange so the employee could catch up on thing he gave up on in sacrificed to the company. However, sometime between the generations, someone rewrote the rules of the game. In today's workforce, you are used and worked until you are too old or too expensive and then laid off just short of being able to qualify for pension benefits. Of course, the business community always puts a nice spin on this phenomenon by calling it re-engineering, reorganization or downsizing.

While these terms are meant to ease the blunt of the act, it ignores a very basic reality. That all those people whose jobs were eliminated were real, with faces, names hopes and dreams. They were people with mortgages to pay, kids to put through college, retirements to save for, and with possible real medical problems. And these people, contrary to popular belief, were not lazy, bad, or unproductive. They worked hard and played by the rules. They paid their taxes and sent their kids to school with the hope that they would achieve a better more easier life than they had, all for a piece of the American Dream. But their employers had something much different in mind.

When it comes to putting employees first, corporate executives used to talk the talk, now they don't even pay lip service to their employees. Very few Chief Executives know or even care about their employees. For there are all beholden to that almighty group known as the Shareholders, which as any first year business student knows, holds his ass, literally in the palm of their hands, for if the profits, and the dividends are not what the shareholders like, The CEO is OUT.

So what is the CEO's main mission, to provide guidance and insight and long term management of the corporation? Hell, no! It is to maximize profits, to put it in Machiavellian terms, "by any means necessary." Access any form of media today, and one will see about a company closing a division or operation and packing up the equipment and moving the whole thing to either China or India to begin operations overseas there. Why? Very Simple. One, Labor costs over in these countries are extremely cheap. A worker over in these countries makes in a month what an American worker makes in one hour. Ok, you say, let's break the Labor unions and force everyone to work for a wage of whatever the company is willing to pay for. Not so fast there folks. We tried that once before, During the beginnings of the industrial revolution in this country would pay workers literally 10 cents an hour for 16 hours a day 6 days a week with no health and safety protections. Of course, the 8 hour work day, health and safety protects in the workplace, no children in the workplace, paid vacations and other benefits were all because organized labor fought, bled and sometimes died for them. I am sad to say, that for most people who have not either grown up in a union household as I did, have not come to understand the saying that a rising tide lifts all boats. That saying does not apply to those occupy to executive suite of some Fortune 500 company, for the simple fact that they have a whole host of accountants and tax attorneys whose sole function is to keep them from paying one thin dime of tax.

Last year, I received a property tax bill from my county. Normally, I would just include it in my next month's mortgage payment to my bank since my taxes and insurance is held in escrow so I do not have to scramble around at Christmas time to pay my taxes. But I digress. My Country tax bill was $1,200 in it was the normal break down of the tax. Library tax, County School tax, Ambulance Tax, County Tax, State Tax, Now since I live in an Independent School district I also pay a tax to them as well... which was $1,000. That is correct, 83% of my tax bill when to my Independent school district, which my father went to, I went to, and both my kids went to. In a following chapter I will discuss the emotional pain and abuse I suffer at the hands of both my peers and teachers at the Independent school ,but that will come later. For now I am just curious to know if I or my parents truly got their money's worth?

Don't get me wrong, I am not anti-tax. Do not lump me in with either the Libertarians or those damn tea-party nut jobs that are nothing short of bat shit crazy. They Love terms like "smaller government, limited governmental intervention. But what these idiots do not realize is when they cut taxes, everyone suffers. Schools do not get maintained. Roads and bridges likewise. We do not invest in our future. As a result, nothing gets repaired, nothing gets fixed. Bridges are in danger of falling, and trains are in danger of derailing. This is a lovely thing considering they are now transporting crude oil though our cities and towns now. But who cares, the railroads and oil companies are making tons or profits, right? Everything is sacrificed for the corporate bottom line. It's alright that corporations and banks are still raking in massive profits while working people are still struggling to make ends meet, right? Of course it is! This is America! To hell with people! Profits over everything! Profits over people!

CHAPTER IV
JOHNNY GOT HIS GUN... AND TOOK IT TO
SCHOOL

This is the one chapter I really wanted discuss in this entire book. Once upon a time we sent Johnny and Susie to school for twelve years of public education and occasional teasing and ridicule from one's peers. And do NOT sit there and attempt to bullshit me by telling me that school, especially high school was the best years of your life, unless of course, you were a jock or a cheerleader, at which time after high you spend the balance of your life reliving those years.

But for the majority of us public education proved to lay the foundations for lifelong learning. Ha, who am I kidding, it was our first exposure to our people in a collective environment, and the dreaded "pecking order." We all know about the pecking order. Let's go down on the farm for a sec, a group of chickens establish dominance over one another by literally "pecking" one another into submission, with the weakest one literally being pecked to death. Now we as humans do not peck our weakest ones to death, we just humiliate them to the point where they either need mental health services or become strippers. Thanks for the business.

When I went to school, we had our problems in schools without question, but nobody, and I do mean nobody would have ever thought about bringing a weapon to school, let alone, shoot and kill a teacher or any other student or school personnel. But that all change on a cold January day in 1993 when a young man in Eastern Kentucky decided to walk into his classroom, take a pistol and take the life of well-loved teacher and janitor. Not only did end their lives, but he took 26 high school students hostage, permanently psychologically scarring an entire community. He is currently serving life in prison with no hope for parole for at least 426 years.

But what this young man also did was set in motion was an unfortunate series of events, namely school shootings and other public shootings, which for the public voices of a short time, then they go back to their sport discussions and other non-important discussions. The problem is that we have in this country are two major problems. First, we have an educational system which preaches excellence while accepts mediocrity. The second is our almost erotic obsession with firearms.

First, let's discuss our educational system. Years ago, we used to be satisfied with teaching our young people the skills necessary for them to get a good paying job and be productive members of society. Now, this country is obsessed with being number one in math and science due to the fact that other countries our literally kicking our assets in those subjects. Problem is, we gave up that when we decided to surrender our manufacturing base in favor of a service oriented economy. Ever since the 1950s, with the advent of "the space race," we decided that this country was falling behind. Now we have decided to test and evaluate student achievement and either reward or penalize schools for how the students perform on those tests. My question is what ever happened to just learning for the simple joy of learning? Oh, I'm sorry, we can't do that. We are getting our assets kicking by the "filling in the appropriate foreign group we are supposed to be afraid of this week."

This is bullshit. We Americans are so damn stupid. We preach and celebrate excellence. Look around, we worship sports and entertainment heroes who are manufactured as "flavors of the month," limited talent and limited staying power. So, in essence, we settle for mediocrity. And we have our talking heads of the news media filling our minds with what we should be afraid of this week. Years ago when I was a child, we would play outside from the moment we got up until the streetlights came on. Now kids will not play alone for fear from their parents that a sexual predator will get them. The message has been sent and is sent: THE WORLD IS NOT SAFE.

For years at school, there were bullies, I was bullied, and my kids were bullied. It was accepted, and in some cases, encouraged by both teachers and administrators due to the fact that those bullies were those higher up on the pecking order. And the encouragement was not necessarily overt, but encouraged by simply by " looking the other way." Why do I point this out? Because I witnessed it, both personally as a child and as an adult, but moreover as a social worker and as a psychotherapist. The beauty of witnessing it as a psychotherapist is I could do something about it. Can you image you joy I felt as a watch the color drain out of someone's face as I just viewed them berate a child and I then told them I was a social worker? Priceless.

Look at the majority of our "in-house" school shooters, starting with our first one back in 1993, the common threat? All were bullied. For a time, school administrators danced around and attempted to "blame the victim," and turn the shooter into some psychopathic monster who did not have any emotional compass, but when the pattern started to develop of average upper middle class white male teenagers from suburbia as the profile as the typical school shooter, people, especially those in mental health, started asking the all-important question, "WHY?"

It turns out that the adolescent subculture was more complex than anyone previous thought. Turns out that from the age of about 8 to 21, American children are being bombarded with messages about gender, sexuality, and gender roles, how manly or how feminine they behave. And are judge accordingly. And I thought I was bullied harshly in school for being the little clumsy fat boy who always fell in mud puddles. I probably had it easy. Nowadays the main point of bullying is regarding a person's sexual orientation. Whether they are gay, straight, or bisexual. Who gives a shit??? I have many gay friends and have no issues with them. They know I am straight, but am the first one to defend them and their rights. But this was not always the case, back in the 1980s, when I wore the mantle of the arch- conservative, I actually opposed gays and gay rights, as well as civil rights. During that time, it was the time, that political correctness was just starting to bloom, and a few conservatives intellectuals and I decided to fight what we thought was the "liberal scourge" in the same spirit of the conservative intellectual, William F. Buckley. I have to admit we did win some battles in our culture war, but we were on the losing side of history, as I soon found out a few years later after I was laid off from a very good paying job at a local steel mill. I was quickly hit with the reality that the Grand Old Party and the conservative movement did not give a shit about the working man or his survival. What compounded that was I had heard that one of my "gay" friends who I had so coldly fought against even the right not to be discriminated against, died from AIDS, alone, and shunned by his family because of his lifestyle. About a year later, another dear friend died of the same dreaded disease, but this time, he was surrounded by family and friends, who eased his pain and discomfort during his final days, but where in denial of his homosexuality. He told them he had contracted the disease while working at a hotel in Seattle from a cut he received unloading some luggage. I chose to remain silent, rather than strip away their Eastern Kentucky innocence.

But now, in the 21st century, we are supposed to no longer bully. Good! It only took us something like 150 years to figure this shit out? Where the fuck was the adults when all this carp was going down? And it suddenly becomes a problem when some kid snaps and decides to turn his classroom into a shooting gallery? Of course it does, because a civil society does not resort to violence, do we?

What a crock of shit! Ever since Columbine, those of us who are considered "expert",(and trust me any licensed mental health professional is recognized as an "expert",) has attempted to lay the blame the lipstick in violence among teens and young adults as violent video games to violence on TV and movies and they have become desensitized to violence making them "natural killers." They argue that they should be placed in more environments. My God, how much more structure do kids need? Children nowadays only have only about three years of development before parents start pushing (yes, I said pushing) them into organized sports, preschool, kindergarten, elementary, middle and high school, after school music and sporting activities, and lest we forget, homework. No wonder children today are fucking depressed, they have no time to be kids, they are more like miniature adults, with planners and scheduling books. Talk about a breeding ground for OCD! No thank you, I will keep the AD/HD I have had since I was a child. And yes, I am unmediated. I prefer it that way, it keeps my mind clear.

Now the second aspect of the lipstick in the rise of violence in this country. Easy access to firearms. Remember, my earlier statement about the experts and violent video games being to blame? I'm calling bullshit on all of my colleagues. They forget the human race is the ultimate predator. How do you think we climbed to the top of the food chain? In fact, we not only kill everything below us on the food chain (sometimes to the point of extinction,) but we have been known to kill our own kind for no apparent reason at all (remember the Holocaust, where six million Jews were slaughtered or the Western Expansion, where countless Native Americans were slaughtered, or even the Great American tragedy, The Civil War as well as slavery, an issue which we are still dealing from its effects.) Of course we don't. We try to forget just how cruel and brutal we can be. But the news just keeps reminding us. A movie theatre in Colorado, a college in Washington, a Law school in Virginia.

Probably, the greatest tragedy of them all was without question, Sandy Hook Elementary School, in Newtown, Connecticut. There a 20 year old young man decided not only to end his mother's life, but traveled to the local Elementary school and proceeded to murder without regard 6 adults and 20 innocent children, all in the first grade, before taking his own life. The young man had a long history of mental illness, but due to the involuntary commitment laws, no one could hospitalize him, because he up to that point had not presented an imminent threat to himself or others, or when the police were called, his family changed their minds and sent them away. If I may take a moment to digress, in the 1960s, just prior to his assassination, John F. Kennedy, had Congress pass laws to encourage the deinstitutionization of the mentally ill, which were housed in state hospitals not fit for most animals to live by providing funding for Community Mental Health Centers. By doing this, the chronically mentally ill could now live and function within the community, with appropriate medical and psychotherapeutic supervision. Now, all went well until the 1980s, when President Reagan, in his efforts of supply-side economics, slashed funding to Community Mental Health Center to the bone. All this in an effort to cut to tax rates from 70% down to 35%. As a result, countless chronically mentally ill did not receive the treatment they desperately needed, they became homeless. State legislatures responded by criminalizing some of those same behaviors. People in an effort to feel better, they turned to illicit substances. Hence substance abuse rates as well increased. As a result, state legislatures increased the penalties for drug crimes, filling up the prisons.

So why haven't I mentioned one word yet about the National Rifle Association yet? Simple, everyone bashes the NRA as a group of self-serving Neo-Con knuckle dragging Neanderthals, which for the most part they are, but this issue is more than just pro-gun ownership rights versus gun control advocates, it is more of a mental health issue. When it is easier to have access to a gun than one has access to affordable and effective mental health care in this country is a travesty. You can have an armed police officer at every school, every public building, every public gathering, and all you will have is the beginnings of a police state. According to Maslow's Hierarchy of Needs, people will trade the higher concepts of freedom and liberty in order to satisfy the basic needs of safety and security. If you look at the events following the September 11th terrorist attacks, Americans were more than willing to trade away some of the freedoms so many of our veterans fought and died to protect in order to have the illusion of feeling safer.

CHAPTER V
GRANDPA, WHERE DID MY FUTURE GO?

I sit in my living room watching my grandson at play. As a doting grandfather, it brings me as a lot of joy. But as a liberal and a social worker, it troubles me as to what future he will inherit when I am no longer around. Given the fact that my generation , the baby boomers, have done everything thing they could to rape and pillage the American society to squeeze every dime of profit out of it by off-shoring jobs, busting unions, and glorifying every Wall Street crook and "job creator" as untouchable.

Back in the day, when the top tax rates hovered around 90%, America boomed. We had money for infrastructure, schools and other needed social programs. Then came the 1980s, or as Ronald Reagan put it, "a new day in America," happened. Laws were passed to cut taxes, unions were busted, businesses were allowed to start moving off shore where they could pay their workers pennies on the dollar compared to American workers. The problem was everyone who was not blue collar did not care. Mainly because they thought they were safe. Wrong! With each downturn in the economy, it appeared that a little more of the middle class disappeared, and more and more people slid further below the poverty line.

As I write this, there are now 3 people competing for every one job. Let that sink in for a moment. Three times the number of workers for every job. What happened? To put it quite simply, we were lulled into a false sense of security. And we took that sense of security and settled into our suburban lifestyles, drinking beer, watching our kids play high school sports, and hang out with the neighbors all the while people we didn't know where plotting our eventual enslavement.

First, it was to make us paranoid. I remember growing up as a child playing outside until the streetlights came on. We knew our neighbors, and you can bet your ads that did something stupid on one end of town, my parents knew about it before I got home. Nowadays, my wife and I would not let our children (and now my grandson) outside our eyesight. Why, because they are sexual predators out there or some other "bad" people who would like nothing less than to do harm to our children or grandchildren. WHAT THE FUCK HAPPENED????

I am quite sure they were evil people back in the day, but everybody knew everyone else and there was more of a sense of community. This is no longer the case. We are lots ourselves into smaller and smaller groups. When this happens, it is harder and Eric to form the bonds of community. Also, we are more polarized than we were years ago. Liberals and conservatives absolutely refuse to see eye to eye on anything. Even now, we do not trust anyone who does not look exactly like we do. Sadly, as long as we judge others more by the color of their skin or the behavior of a select few of a particular group, we will never truly develop as a population.

Secondly, as members of the Caucasian race, we feel a sense of superiority. This is not a recent development. If you examine human history since the fall of the Roman Empire, you will see the behavior of the Caucasian race towards members of other races to be rather cruel and even barbaric. On Election Day 2012, my father and I were having a conversation regarding the election and the candidates, Mitt Romney and President Barack Obama, the classic matchup between a rich old white guy and a liberal. My dad made the statement that the white race throughout history has been "just evil." He went on the say that what they could not conquer and enslave, they killed. I couldn't have agreed with him more.

Yet today, we still see the same behaviors from white Americans. They want our borders closed, not our northern border with Canada, but a southern border with Mexico and other Spanish speaking countries. It does not matter that they provide a large number of the labor for our agricultural, food service, and several other industries which Americans would never dare soil their hands to do. It is the very simple fact that their skins are darker than ours and they speak a different language than us. Sadly, they are fighting a losing battle. By the year 2040, white Americans will be in the minority. This immigrants are not leeches or parasites, taking what they can off the American social safety net. These are hard working men and women only looking for the same better life what a lot of American ancestors did 100 to 150 years ago. America: the land of opportunity. BULLSHIT!

We in America have developed the attitude much as the Germans did during the Weimar Republic in between World War I and the Rise of the Nazi Party. Our economy is shot to hell, and while we do not have runaway inflation, we have a horrible job market, skyrocketing debt, and a mistrust of other races, especially those whose skin is darker than ours.

But I digress, we have the ability to generate large sums of cash for both state and federal coffers through reinstatement of the tax structures of the 1930s to the 1970s. The grand experiment of supply side economics where if you cut taxes on the wealthy and corporations. The thought behind this idea is that their treasuries would overflow to the point that it would " trickle down" to the rest of us. I am still waiting for the Damn trickle. And so are a bunch of other American families.

John Maynard Keynes, the father of Keynesian economic policy, stated the best way to stimulate economic growth was through governmental spending, as they are the only ones who have the only ability to generate massive spending on a very large scale. Now my conservative friends would argue that bigger government is socialistic, and runs against the grain of our rugged individualism which "made this country great." Many times they complain that this country is rapidly turning into a "Nanny state," taking care of its population from the cradle to the grave. Sadly, the nations of Norway and Sweden have got the "Nanny state" concept right. Education, even college is free. Teachers are paid well. There is no such thing as student loans and those who do not qualify for college are taught a trade. Hmmmm. Are taxes high? Of course, but the wages are high enough that even with high taxes there is enough money left over for people to live comfortably. Not only does this governmental spending drive conservatives bat shit crazy, combine this with the fact that Keynes was gay absolutely drives them insane.

The sad thing about America is we have several issues in our country which are like the elephant in the room. We still cling to the pipe dream that if we work hard enough, we will be successful. As for my personal experience, I have worked hard ever since I was 18. I have been a grocery store clerk, a bouncer in a gentleman's club, a steelmaker, a security guard, a comptroller for a multi-million dollar construction company, a psychotherapist, a supervisor, and an administrator. I have led people and projects. I have had extreme successes as well as dismal failures. Yet, I am not wealthy. Why? I have three college degrees. Two Masters Degrees. I have an IQ that qualifies me to be in MENSA. YET I AM NOT WEALTHY. Why? One simple word. LIFE. While my wife and I work hard, we have both been victims of office politics, co-workers with their own agendas or wanting to "make their bones," or bosses with whom one minute you are their right hand and the next you are a pariah. We've lost jobs, been laid off, lost our positions due to funding cuts, or just been terminated for whatever reason. Yet we are always able to find some form of employment, but being a social worker does not pay well. Now I am not complaining about my career choices, but businesses, particularly those in the human services industry, they need to realize if they want to keep good employees, they should hire the best and pay them like they are worth it.

Ever since the 1980's, we in this country have been working more and more and getting paid less for it. Productivity has skyrocketed while wages has pretty much stagnated for the middle and lower classes. Hell, the minimum wage has not been raised since the 1990s, yet prices, especially those for gas, food, you know, the necessities of life, continue to increase. Is it not a shame that Wal-Mart, and the Walton family control more wealth than 40% of other Americans, while their employees struggle to get by on public assistance? I find it a crying shame, not only as a social worker, but as a human being, that others in the workforce do not bring home enough pay to put a roof over their heads, food in both them and their children's bellies and clothes on their backs. Maslow, in his hierarchy of needs explained that a person must take care of basic necessities before take care of other levels of the hierarchy (such as getting an education, etc.)

Now I know the first words out of conservative's mouth, "Raising the minimum wage will kill jobs and throw us into massive unemployment." My reply to them to show me one time, just one time, when an increase in the minimum wage has caused a downturn in the economy. Please go and investigate this, take all the time you need. I'll wait.

Hopefully by now you've realized that there was no downturn in the economy after any increase in the minimum wage. So why is there such outrage over raising the minimum wage? Simple. Greed. The more money paid to employees, the less available for the owners to pocket. Even though it has been proven time and again that when more money people have, the more money they will spend. This would be a boost to the economy. Instead of being a job killer as predicted by the conservatives, it would actually create jobs, just as Keynes advocated. The conservative movement will never ever embrace the concept of demand side economics due to the fact that it demands an increase in the size of government. That, and combined with the fact Keynes was gay also causes most conservatives to blow a mental gasket!

You see there are three types of conservatives: economic conservatives, social conservatives, and the notorious Tea-baggers. Economic and social conservatives I'll get to a little later. But for the moment, let us focus our attention upon that is called The Tea Bagger. They are a blend of both a social and economic conservative, yet they are too dumb to understand the complex social issues they so diligently protest against. They are constantly supporting candidates who vote against them and their own self-interests while making them think they are actually doing them a favor.

Remember just a few paragraphs ago I pointed out an America of the 1950s and early 1960s where the white male was the Supreme Being. That is the world the Tea Bagger longs for. The social norms of the 1950s, the economic norms of the roaring 20s, and a return to the labor. Conditions of the 1890s. The rich economic conservatives have used the Tea Bagger lack of sophistication and fear of knowledge to their advantage by convincing them that they are actually on their side. This is probably the greatest con game ever pulled off in the history of mankind. To actually fool people into voting against their own best interests. They talk about "welfare queens" driving around in Cadillacs, instantly invoking racist undertones which have been present since the reconstruction era in the south. They invoke the sanctity of human life in regards to abortion, but when they are born into a poor family who has to depend upon food stamps (or SNAP benefits as they called now,) they are basically shit out of luck. The neo-cons view these children as lazy or somehow unworthy of assistance due to their circumstances. However, I stand before you and say that even I and my family have had to turn to public assistance once to help make ends meet and put food on the table for us and our kids. You do what you have to do sometimes to feed you family. Was I embarrassed? Hell, no? Do you know why? BECAUSE I FUCKING PAID TAXES, THAT'S WHY! The Neo conservatives argue that churches and non-profits will pick up the slack if we get rid of the social safety net. I'm gonna call bullshit on that on as well due to the fact that churches have gotten away from caring for the sick and poor and rather building these huge Mega-Churches. Nothing in this world burns me up more than to think that the church has not only wants what is God's, but they also want what is Cesar's!

CHAPTER VI

JUST LOOK FOR THE UNION LABEL

You know, I have a lot of acquaintances who believe sincerely that we have evolved sufficiently as a society that we have no need for any reason for organized labor in the workplace. I, again, am going to call bullshit on that one. My logic behind this. First off, I have worked in both union and non-union workplaces. Unionized ones were ones were you felt a lot safer in, were there was never this nagging fear of accidentally pissing off the boss . But in my journeys, I have found places where a union simply does not work.

One place for example, is a call center of a fortune 100 company I work for currently. I shall not name the company. But before most union folks start foaming at the mouth over my last statement let me defend it.. The company uses pure metrics to make decisions. In other words, it is or it isn't, there is no in between. While this works most of the time, it does not take into account a lot of the gray areas in which human behavior fall in. Not all human behavior can be measured nor can it be computed down into nicest figures on a spread sheet.

While unions have taken a serious beating in the past 30 years due to the advent of right to work laws and a general lack of knowledge of the younger generation concerning the past struggles of the previous generations to secure a lot of the workplace freedoms most of us take for granted. Things such as the 40 hour work week, workers compensation, no child labor, and many other things which union men and women fought, struck and even some of them died to achieve.

I have talked too many of my Neo-Con friends who are constantly telling me that unions are old, outdated and are no longer needed in the American workplace. I counter their argument with the fact that unions are needed now more than ever. Primarily due to the vast amount of income inequality in this country. Of course they look at me like I have three sucking heads when I say that because due to the fact they all think they are doing well making 75K to 100K a year and they live in a nice house in the suburbs and their kids go to excellent schools and the future looks absolutely rosy. But what they fail to realize, again, is what I always see, the nasty underbelly of life. The unforeseen things, such as illness, injury, layoff or terminations. A big trick in the late 80s and 1990s was employees who had 20 to 25 year's service under their belts, suddenly find them downsized as companies merged or cut staff in an effort to become "leaner and meaner."

Suddenly these bastions of middle management found themselves like the poor blue collar schmucks they laughed at and scorned in the late 70s and early 80s. Unemployed, without prospect, without hope. Talk out schadenfreuden. I am quite sure many a blue collar worker had a good laugh over their beers when they saw white collar workers getting the same treatment they are used to getting. While it was neither funny nor enjoyable to see another human being to see another human being suffer the same fate as so many others, it did one a gentle reminder that in today's economy, no one is safe.

To say that I come from a union family is probably an understatement. My great-grandfather belonged to the UTU. My grandfather, my uncle and myself were members of the United Steelworkers of America, and my father was a member first of the United Transportation Union and later the Brotherhood of Locomotive Engineers. Even my son was a member of the United Food and Commercial Workers. So my respect and my support for working people and organized labor are pretty much in my DNA.

Even my daughter, at the age of 6 weeks of age, walked the picket line with her grandfather and me during a nationwide railroad strike in 1990.

There was once union a time in this nation's history (during the late 1940s to the 1950s,) where organized labor enjoyed its highest levels of membership. And the middle class in this nation flourished. People who were once so poor they had to struggle to put food on the table now had the capacity to not only put food on the table but also had the ability to give themselves and their children opportunities to go to college. This caused a great shift in the socio-economic structure of the country. That scared the living daylights out of the "elites." Who viewed the up and comers as "the great unwashed." I have gone to school, worked with and socialized with these same folks I am talking about. They have a completely different mindset than I and the majority of people I know have.

First off, they have an unrealistic expectation of preserving the status quo. So naturally they vote Republican. They are also have a very narrow very of the world in an "I got mine, fuck you," mentality. They believe that there work is more important, adds more value, is of greater impact than a man who punches a time clock or gets his hands dirty. This is a very dangerous attitude to have, particularly since those wealthy bastards would be the first ones to die in the event of financial collapse. You see, some 65% of our money is electronic. That's right. There is a good chance that your money and everyone else's, it just bits of computer code. When I found that out, it literally blew my mind. So you're saying big deal, what does that have to do with me. The reason it has every reason to do with you is money.

But in all seriousness, take a good hard look around. Notice lately that they gap between the rich and the poor keeps getting wider and wider as the middle-class keeps falling further and further behind? Let me put it another way, during the 1950s,when tax rates for the top incomes were at 90%, the pay difference between the CEOs and their workers was about 30x. Nowadays, the difference is more like 300%. Now the first thing my Neo-Con friends like to scream is class warfare. Sorry, this is not class warfare when one part of the population has vulgar displays of wealth while the other part of the population can nearly afford transportation. Something is definitely wrong.

We used to be a manufacturing powerhouse. You name it, we made it. But you know what? The corporations figured out back in the 1980s that they could acquire a huge amount of debt, buy another company, cut the workforce (mostly the blue collar with a few lower and middle managers mixed in,) sell off parts of the company, raid the pensions of the retirees, take a huge chunk of cash and move on the next victim. And these fucking assholes were held as the awesome businessmen and women for being the experts of being "making companies lean and mean." It got to the point that the business world thought they had to be so lean and mean their competitors would be pissing in their pants with fear. Please. There were a lot of people died from stress and overwork during that period of time due to all those behaviors. Going back to Maslow's hierarchy of needs, while we had so many,(the wealthy,) working hard in the esteem level, we had the middle and poorer classes struggling in the basic needs stage.

So why am I such a fan of unions? Simple. Unions level the playing field for all workers. They also advocate for things that humanize workers. If it was not for unions, workers would basically be treated just like machinery, if it breaks down in any way shape or form, it is discarded and replaced. Well, that is rapidly becoming that way. It has been reported over the past few winters workers actually have chosen to go to work with the flu and other diseases rather than stay home and recover. Strange that the United States is the only industrialized country in the world the does not have mandated time off for maternity leave or vacations such as countries in Europe. Even though studies have proven the European factories and workers are far more productive than their American counterparts. Oh, and did I mention the just about every government in Europe is either socialist or socialist leaning? And that the average work week in European work week is 32 to 36 hours compared to 40 to 50 in the good ole USA? I know, I know, you will argue that Americans are more industrious and Europeans are just a bunch of slackers. But why is it that Europeans work to live and Americans live to work? We have so much of our live, our self-worth, and our souls tied up in our jobs that when something happens to us or our jobs we are devastated.

So are unions outdated. NO! People can and will only take so much self-abuse before they start pushing back. If you are a student of history like I am, you will realize these times are very similar to the roaring 20s leading up to the Great Depression. But the major difference between now and then is that back then people had the knowledge and abilities to live off the land. People farmed, raised cows, chickens, maybe a couple of goats. They planted a garden, canned and pickled vegetables. Butchered hogs fattened by food scraps. People fixed things rather than throwing them away. The wealthy believe that they are better than the rest of us. Therefore they believe that they are immune from the coming storm. To paraphrase George R.R. Martin, "winter is coming." Are you prepared? I fear that we in this country are not prepared for what in coming economically. People are ill prepared for any major economic downturn. That is why any time when I hear of a state passing right to work legislation or anything to undermine workers, including the argument against raising the minimum wage, I cringe. Because, they always argue for tax cuts for the wealthy using the argument that a rising tide lifts all boats, but they never use the same argument when it comes to raising the minimum wage. Ever stop to ask why? Because it helps poor people that's why! Our country worships three things more than anything. Money, youth, and beauty. Since World War II, our culture has been obsessed with those three things. Look at Hollywood and Wall Street, both are extremes of a different kind. But both are artificial and a facade.

So what do we do? All rush out and join a union? No. But, do support union made and built items. Look for Made in America items. If you see a picket line, honor it. Donate your time to food kitchens or items to your local food pantries to help those less fortunate. Donate to your favorite charity, not necessarily money, but time, gently used clothes and items also prove beneficial as well. Remember, no one is safe in today's economy from the downturns. I am not an economist. My observations are just that, my observations.

CHAPTER VII

MILITIAS: CHOCK FULL O' NUTS

You know every time a democrat (liberal) President is elected, it seems that there is an upswing in the appearance of right wing "nut"groups, and militia groups formed in an effort to protect their freedoms. They constantly believe that the government is coming to take our guns, Wisk us off to reeducation camps and turn America into a communist country. This is the biggest crock of bull shit I have ever heard. It was done in the Clinton administration in the 1990s and is being done during now while President Barack Obama is in Office. But Obama is a different story. The say that the President is not eligible for his office because he was born in Kenya. This is also is crock of shot due to the fact that his mother was AMERICAN, which means he could have been born on Mars and still be an American citizen. This only thing President Obama is guilty of is that he is African-American.

I believe this is the main reason for the rise of those militia groups. Liberals have this nasty habit of advocating for equality for all. Women, African-Americans, Latinos, Native Americans and the poor Liberals believe that all Americans have a place at the table and should have the opportunities that make America great. However, the conservatives believe that only a narrow few should have that opportunity. And those are usually white, male Anglo-Saxon, Protestant as well as middle to old age. Kind of the people who are active in militia groups.

They do not like the idea of equality for all. Mainly due to the fact that they adhere to the old ideas from the antebellum era in which white males occupied the top of the social ladder, no matter how rich or poor they were. Women, while being thought of just a little higher than chattel property, are treated as little children, not being capable of making their own decisions. Minority groups are segregated in an atmosphere of "separate but equal," even though if we remember during the Jim Crow era, segregation was separate but not equal. I find it hard to fathom why people would like to live in a nation where a one whole segment of its population is relegated to less than full citizenship.

Of course now conservatives are railing against people coming from countries such as El Salvador and Guatemala, the majority of which are minors traveling alone or mothers traveling with their children. People want to go to the border armed to the teeth to " keep them feriners out." What the fuck has happened to my country? We used to help immigrants come into and integrate into our culture. But this is no longer the case. I know, back in our history we did not consider Irish people or Italians as "white people," but we eventually learn to accept them into our melting pot culture. Now my question is this," Why do we have such an avoidance to accept African-American or Latinos into are culture as well? Is it because their skin is darker than ours?

Have you ever been walking down the street and seen a black Latino man walking toward you? What do you do? Do you cross the street to avoid them? Avoid eye contact or grip your purse a little tighter? Racism is so pervasive in our culture we almost do not think about it. It impacts us from our schools all the way up to our criminal justice system.

With our schools, we see both public inner city and many suburban schools which were built in the 60s and 70s are slowly falling apart while upper middle and upper class schools continue to turn out top notch students. They created "charter schools" in which people who can afford them can send their children (mostly white affluent families,) in an effort to get them into the best colleges. Furthermore, there is an increase in religious schools as well. Both of these creatures attempt to siphon off tax dollars from local school systems, all of which is supported by the GOP governors and legislatures of these states. It is all an effort to reinstitute the same "separate but unequal" systems which was prevalent in the Jim Crow era. Also, most of these behaviors are occurring in the states of the old Confederacy. And immediately after the 2012 election, those same states started talking about secession. Too bad that question was already settled in 1865, when Robert E. Lee surrendered at Appomattox Court House.

Unfortunately, the old south never truly got over losing the Civil War. They never truly got over having their entire social culture ripped away from them. A society where no matter how low on the socio-economic ladder a white man was he was always above the black man. Even my grandfather, the man who, along with my father, instilled in me my work ethic and a great deal of my knowledge, was probably the most racist man I have met. He was not above dropping the N-word on a right regular basis. In fact, he would tease us grandchildren that he would, "Go over to Ironton and find him a little N*gger baby to be his buddy." We would always squeal and say "No Papaw,no!" And he would always chuckle and laugh. As a child, I did not realize the impact of those statements. But I also realize that he was born in 1916, and grew up during the Jim Crow era, so racism was pretty much an accepted part of life. I always say you can not judge the past by today's standards.

I have a confession to make, during the 1980s, I was very conservative. So conservative I made Rush Limbaugh look.like a flaming liberal. When the University of Kentucky was deciding whether or not to divest its holdings in companies which did business in South Africa during the era of Apartheid, I was one of the leading voices in opposition to the move. My argument was that it was "a bad business move," to divest, especially when most of these companies were Fortune 500 companies. Needless to say, we lost that battle, but looking back, I'm glad we failed. I made a lot of enemies during that time, and for that I'm sorry. I can always use the excuse the foolishness of youth, but I will mark it down as the foolishness of being an ignorant ass conservative.

But I digress. If we are ever to progress as a culture, we have to start having a serious discussion about race in this country. Not just about the African-American experience, but also Native American, Hispanic, as well as now since we started the "war on terror," the Muslim population in this country. Do we seek to learn about other cultures? Do we seek to understand other cultures? I would venture to say the 10% of us do not take the time to learn about our neighbors, what they are all about or who they are. As a result, we are no longer one nation, but we are a fragmented society. As pointed out in the 2008,2010, and 2012 elections, our nation is almost split 50% liberal and 50% conservative. And since we now have such news outlets like Fox News, CNN and MSNBC filling our brains full of filtered news for either political leanings, we are basically at a political stalemate. And we constantly use the race card as a stirring point to fire up our respective political bases.

Let's take a look for a minute at Florida, usually where old white people go to die. Now it has one of the most liberal gun laws called "Stand your Ground," a person, armed with gun, who is threatened does not have the right to defend themselves with deadly force rather than retreating. In Kentucky, we have something similar, called "the Castle doctrine," based on the principle that a man's home is his castle and he has the right to defend it with deadly force. But in this case, a 17 year old young man named Trevon Martin, an African-American honor student who was walking to his father's house with a can of soda and some Slim-Jims, was shot and killed by a wanna be cop named George

Zimmerman. Mr. Zimmerman was nothing more than a vigilante. But he used the "Stand your Ground" defense to basically get away with murder. But a few weeks later in the same state, a 17 year old African-American young man was shot and killed by a white man who felt threatened because the young men were playing their car stereo too loud. However, when African-American attempts to apply the same defense, it does not apply. When an African-American woman fired a shot into the ground while her abusive boyfriend was threatening her, she received 20 years in prison. Do we see a pattern here? I thought justice was blind? I suppose not. If it is, it is not color blind.

Look at our correctional institutions. We in the United States, the land of the free and home of the brave, has the largest number of incarcerated individuals of ANY industrialized country in the world. The majority of which are either African-American or Latinos. To this old social worker, sounds a bit like state sponsored slavery to me. But I am not the only one who views this as an injustice. New York State by a group of concerned citizens is working hard to do away with the use of solitary confinement as a form of punishment. However, there are those in law enforcement and corrections who feel that those incarcerated should be treated less than human.in the South (there we go again,) we are seeing a resurgence in chain gangs and other forms of inmate labor as a way to reduce savings to the state and making money for these institutions. We also have entering the arena for profit prisons, giving raise to what is being called the "prison industrial complex."

Now, given that the majority of incarcerated are minorities, which usually vote Democratic, it would appear that there is an effort to disenfranchise a good deal of minorities by simply making them convicted felons. One doesn't have to worry about minorities voting if they can't vote now do we? Of course, ever since the end of the civil war, our prison populations have always been tipped heavily toward minorities. I am curious to know once whites fall in minority status if that will change? Then again, I wonder I wonder if the old rich white men have read the handwriting on the wall and are terrified of the future, which would explain why they are desperately trying everything to hold onto every little shred of power he can while he can. People are a funny lot, for over 1000 years, Europeans attempted to mold the world in their image, but killing and enslaving others, some in the name of riches, and others in the name of religion. Of course Africans and Asians have just as brutal and just as gory a history as Europeans and Americans do, it's just we have taken ours to an art form.

I look at my grandson Luke, he has no hate and no basis. He sees everyone has an equal, a friend. In fact he will run up to kids on the playground and ask them, " Do you want to be my friend?" Such innocence. In a way, I am envious of him. He has a very innocent view of the world. In his world everyone is honest, happy and polite. Free from cynicism and brutality that modern day life brings to human beings. I saw that same innocence evaporate from my children over the years just as it disappeared from me many years ago. I know that in position has a social worker I always looked for the good in most people, but I brought a great deal of cynicism with me to the job when I entered the profession.

CHAPTER VIII
RIGHT IS RIGHT AND LEFT IS WRONG, OR IS IT?

People like being comfortable. That is why the Right has been so successful in their earnings gains in the body politic. Their message has been the same 1980, "God, Guns, and Gays." Once upon a time, Republicans and Democrats used to actually work together for the benefit of the country. Now it is about power and holding power. And holding those out of power hostage to the whims of those in power. But now it is more like a battle royale for ultimate control of how America will be.

We used to think that we were the top of the heap. Economically, militarily, educationally. At least that what we were told in school. Our high school counselors, if we were smart enough, guided us toward college, those who were not well, there was always the military. They did not even bother mentioning the possibility of going to trade school to become a welder, plumber, or an electrician. Heaven forbid an American child would ever get his hands dirty doing manual labor. We are American, the land of money. The land that worshipped the all mighty dollar.

But look what happened, was all of us, myself included, is now saddled with a huge amount of student loan debt that we have little or no hope of ever paying back. As it stands currently, Americans currently owe over one TRILLION dollars in student loan debt. Debt which causes them to work on fear . Fear of never challenging anything of the system. The suddenly become mindless drones, only working. Never taking any type of advocacy in any types of cause which might bring about worthwhile change.

During the time immediately after World War II came the largest generation that America had ever witnessed. The Baby Boomers, my generation. Those of us born between January 1, 1946 and December 31, 1964, has the benefit of being the best educated, most consumption driven generation ever in American history. We have seen more, done more, had more opportunities and have squandered those opportunities than any generation in history.

Case in point, health care. The United States is the only industrialized nation which does not have a centralized healthcare system. Now granted this decision was made back in 1947, when centralized health care seemed to be a "socialistic" idea. Why does the United States have such an aversion to making health care a basic human right? Very simple. Healthcare makes up 17% of the American economy. You have billions of dollars going to doctors, hospitals, insurance companies, and the pharmaceutical industry. There is no motivation to change.

Just as in our manufacturing sector, during the 1950s and 1960s, 90% of my toys and stuff we bought were made in America. If it said, Made in Japan or Made in China, it was junk. We took pride in our products we made. And our moms and dads made good livings and raised us up to have the same expectations of life in America. But in the 1970s, something changed, the attitudes of Americans changed we lost our "can do" spirit. We started making less than our best. The Japanese and Germans started making better quality more affordable goods than we could. Suddenly, everyone started buying imported goods. About that same time, the availability of credit boomed. We no longer become frugal as the generation which lived through the Great depression was, we became a nation of conspicuous consumers. While this is not necessarily a bad thing, we are started the shift for a manufacturing based economy to a service oriented economy. While services such as doctors, attorneys, and stockbrokers made excellent compensation, others on the end of the spectrum, the janitors, food service workers and store clerks were stuck on the minimum wage end of the scale. But every time there is a call for a raise in the minimum wage, both conservatives and small business owners scream that such a raise would kill their business and possibly lead them to cut back or even close.

If you listen to the conservative talk heads, America has lost its moxie. We can't accomplish what we used to do, invent and simply things. We need to take ownership of our future. I know for a fact our system has plenty of defects, defects which needs some form of activism in order to change. Even though I am no longer a practicing social worker, I still take a keen interest in politics. I read several newspapers and magazines, all with differentiating opinions. I listen to various views on topics of the day. I am an informed opinionated individual. Now instead of sitting around, watching ESPN, trying to figure out who is going to be taken in the first round of the draft, or when getting the newspaper going straight to the sports section, take a few minutes to actually read the news and absorb the information there. I know I might be asking a lot but for God's sake, get off your collective asses and develop a fucking opinion about the world around you.

Those in power hope that people do not develop an opinion. Alan Greenspan, former chairman of the Federal Reserve, had a theory of Salary Uncertainty, which has been economic policy of this country for the past 30 years. With it, employees do not ask for wages or raises. They work and toil harder and harder to fuel the economic engine of consumerism. But there is a fly in the ointment, without a steady increase in wages, people lose their buying power. Instead of purchasing iPhones and Michael Korrs handbags, they are using their wages to buy things like food, clothing and rent or the mortgage. Eventually, the economy grinds to slow crawl.

So what do conservatives do, they stoke fear. Fear of the unknown. The fear of immigration, gays, background checks for gun ownership. The fear that they wake up one morning that the illusion of the American dream is gone. Is it gone? No, not yet. But people have to pay attention. Because for the past 30 years, the American people have been asleep in the wheel. And in the meantime, those in power and those who operate our economy have taken our hopes, our dreams and sold them for short term profit. Sad, even the Japanese during the 1980s was amazed the amazed that Americans were so willing to sell their birthright when Americans were selling companies to them right, left and sideways.

Normally, a merger was to bring to like forces in businesses together to enhance both and make them better. During the 80s and 90s, not so much. The point of modern mergers was to gain and hold market share, to the point of being almost being a monopoly, lending itself for the maximizing of profit. Of course, the conservatives preach the profit motive like it is it's own religion. To the best of my knowledge, America is the only country on the face of the earth in which politics, economics, religion, and morality have combined into this strange mutant. If you are rich, you must be this great morally upstanding person. If you are poor, then you must be some shiftless, lazy, worthless bum, unworthy of any assistance on any level. Kind of like the Elizabethan poor laws developed in the 1600s in England. It decided who was to be considered "worthy" and "unworthy" poor. They are trying to assign such designations today. Republicans in Congress today have pretty much decided that ALL poor are unworthy due to the fact they wish to create a society based on an Ayn Rand novel (please, I waited nine chapters before mentioning that insane Capitalist, even though she collected Social Security in her old age.) They want to create a society where the rich are greatly rewarded and the balance of the population is left to fend for themselves. Any Rand advocated pure capitalism, with no rules, regulation, or interference from the government. The Republicans currently in Congress are hell bent in repealing every social program and environmental regulation made since the 1970s to make the climate better for " job creators." Some of our elected officials have even proposed right-to-work legislation to ensure that organized labor would be broken to the point that workers would be returned to a further state of wage slavery. No voice. No protections. Just work until you drop. So if you think your voice and vote doesn't matter, think again.

But there is hope, there are spots in this country where workers are waking up to the reality that they can make a difference. When workers narrowly defeated an attempt by the United Auto Workers to organize a Volkswagen plant in Tennessee, partially due to negative union propaganda by both the Governor and a U.S. Senator saying that if a union came in VW would not add another product line to the Tennessee plan. What they failed to plan on was the German commitment of inclusion of workers in their decision making process. The UAW organized another union, Local 42 (selected due to Jackie Robinson's number,) at the Tennessee plant, they were proud of the fact that they will be producing a new VW model, contrary to what the Republican elected officials told both the VW workers and the public. A politician lie? Please.

What we now have in this country is a blatant attack on the working class and the poor, by the rich and powerful. Why? Why not. You have an economic bully who wants not only his money, but the money of those who can least afford to lose it. The poor, the elderly,and the disadvantaged. Of course the first thing out of

Republicans mouths is if they are able bodied, they should work. Fine. But what if they suffer from a chronic physical or mental illness which prevents them from working. I suffer from a back injury I received on the job and have had two major surgeries to get me back to being able to work. One was a Lumbar fusion which sucked, but it got me back on my feet. The second was an installation of a spinal cord stimulator, which sucked worse. But luckily, I was able to return to work, not as a psychotherapist, my neuro-surgeon said that was out, so I took my talents and now work in a call center. It's a living, and it's a good living.

The interesting thing about working in my call center is that I am making the same rate of pay I was when I was a steelworker 25 years ago. Now 25 years ago, I was a newlywed, gas was $1.50 a gallon, everything was cheaper and my wife and I thought we were rolling in the dough. However, in 2014, the same payday doesn't seem to go as far. Possibility because I now have to pay for my own health insurance (provided and paid for my employer,) and pay into my own retirement (also provided by my employer.) Plus I also by disability and life insurance for myself, spouse and children, something I had never thought about 25 years ago. I suppose many of you make the same expenditures out of your paychecks.

So with dealing with the ever present shrinking paycheck and the daily condition called life, what's a person to do? I do not have a solid answer. I suppose we could go back to frugality previous generations adhered to years ago. Or we could continue on our current course of debt and living paycheck to paycheck. As for me, I attempt to squirrel away a little away each payday. It's not much, but I always have a little bit for a rainy day or in the event of an emergency. Trust there is always an emergency that pops up unexpectedly, from a blown tire to a clogged sink.

CHAPTER IX

AFTER ALL IS SAID AND DONE...

Finally! We have reached the end of this journey into my first foray into writing a book. Mostly I wrote this for fun, but also I have toys with the idea of writing a book for some 30 odd years. But being someone who really does not think I have anything worthwhile to say, well not anything anyone really wants to hear anyway. You see we are bombarded daily with enough crap from the corporate media and it's TV offspring, that our minds are numb. No wonder we have a very bad habit of turning in "Jersey Shore" and tune out the nightly news. We are more interested in TMZ than in reading a newspaper. People feel helpless and hopeless. As a result, we go to Starbucks to get going and take Ambien to go to sleep. Possibility that is why Prozac is the most researched and prescribed medication in the history of mankind. Here in the United States we are all work and little to no play. We do NOT have a system of mandated days off nor do we have any type of paid type of paternity/maternity leave. We Americans are expected to literally work ourselves into the grave to feed the Capitalist Corporate behemoth. As a result, our health and well-being suffers. Our children suffer, as we delegate surrogates to instill our morals and ethics, but instead they our taught to be good little drones, never questioning, never deviating, just working, working working.

I am not a foe of work, in fact I believe it builds character. But we need balance in life. In Europe, people there take time to enjoy life and each other. As a result, they have less stress, longer life spans and more overall happiness. Not a bad combo, you think? I know, I know....'Merica. LOVE IT OR LEAVE IT. Please, if you have that narrow minded view regarding the world we live in, GET THE FUCK OFF MY PLANET! You have no business complaining about the situation you have helped cause. That is why I have gave this book this title, due to the fact we are ALL guilty of being asleep at the wheel while our American Dream was slowly taken away from ourselves, our children, and our grandchildren. We now have to all have to work a lot harder, than our parents did for a smaller piece of the economic pie. And even when we attempt to better ourselves, we become like hamsters stuck on the wheel. Running constantly, but never truly making any progress.

That is why I became a Progressive. In the hope, that my small actions would help working men and women, school aged children, the elderly to have a better world. But like so many advocates before me, I am probably whistling in the graveyard. For we share responsibility for the shape our economy as well as our economic future, not only for ourselves but for our fellow man. ALL OUR HANDS ARE STAINED.

Ok, now that I have that off my chest. I invite you to leave feedback, good or bad. And who knows if I like (or really dislike, snicker,) what you say I might reply.

For a better world.

-FIN-